Scottish History

Photographs by
Colin Baxter

Text by
Chris Tabraham

LOMOND BOOKS

EDINBURGH · SCOTLAND

Scottish History

Scotland BC

Mankind first set foot on the land now called Scotland more than 9000 years ago. What name they gave to the densely forested landscape they encountered, where reindeer grazed and polecat prowled, is a mystery, like so much of their story. They were a restless folk, moving about the land, never far from shore, in the relentless search for food, remaining in one place only long enough to leave behind the odd camp-fire and the remains of their last meal.

For 3000 years generations of these mesolithic hunters and gatherers roamed the land. Slowly the desire to put down roots began to take hold. The wild landscape was becoming home to them, as they returned to old and familiar haunts. Their primitive stone tools, capable only of catching fish and game, developed into implements able to tame the environment and till the soil. By 4000 BC our stone-age ancestors had become Scotland's first farmers.

The more settled communities abandoned their nomadic way of life and began to build more permanently. The remains of their endeavours – their houses and fields, ceremonial places and burial tombs – are

LOCH AN EILEIN, Rothiemurchus, Strathspey, with a remnant of Caledonian pine forest.

IONA ABBEY, Argyll. (opposite) The lovingly restored medieval abbey stands on the spot where St Columba set up his monastery on the island of Iona in AD 563.

*SKARA BRAE, Orkney.
North-west Europe's best
preserved prehistoric village
was inhabited 5000 years
ago, before the Egyptian
pyramids and Stonehenge
were built.*

scattered across the land, from the Mull of Galloway to the northernmost
tip of Shetland.

But it is in Orkney, amid the enchanting ruins of the neolithic village
of Skara Brae, inhabited for more than 600 years around 3000 BC, that
we perhaps get closest to their world, so different from our own, and yet
with an eerily familiar feel, particularly those cosy homes, with their beds
and dressers.

More difficult to comprehend are their great ceremonial circles and
monumental tombs. What they did inside the stone circle called the
Stones of Stenness, or who they buried within the great stone tomb of
Maes Howe, are more of those eternal mysteries, but their very
construction, in an age which had yet to witness Stonehenge or the
mighty pyramids of Egypt, is powerful proof of an intelligent people
with a strong sense of community.

The climate in those far-off times was comfortably warm, sufficient
to enable wheat to flourish in furthest Shetland and exotic fish to swim
in the seas. But a decline set in as the second millenium BC drew to a
close, and so, apparently, did man's ability to live in peace with his

*THE STONES OF
STENNESS, Orkney.
A great ceremonial meeting
place for prehistoric
Orcadians.*

MOUSA BROCH,
Shetland.
The best preserved broch in
all Scotland, on the now
uninhabited island of Mousa.

THE CUP-AND-RING-
MARKED ROCKS AT
ACHNABRECK, Argyll,
are amongst the finest and
most elaborate examples of
prehistoric rock-art in
Scotland.

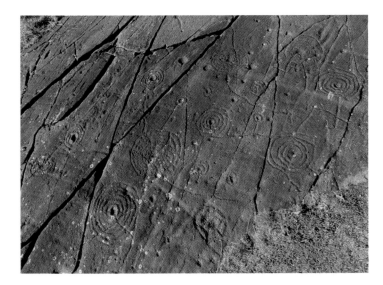

neighbour. The skill of working copper metal, introduced from Europe about 2000 BC, came to be used not just to create better tools and more attractive jewellery but to produce weapons. Perhaps the cooler, wetter weather, which encouraged the growth of peat and reduced the amount of cultivatable land, placed undue pressures on communities, leading to greater conflict.

The first truly defensive structures, hillforts, appeared in the seventh century BC, about the same time that iron-working technology arrived, innovations that have been taken as proof of the coming of the Celts from eastern Europe. But new-fangled ideas can as effectively be spread by a few folk as by a mass influx of people, and there is evidence that the Celtic language was being spoken long before this by our first neolithic farmers.

Some hillforts were sprawling tribal centres, others were more modest, the homes of just a few families. As the pre-Christian world drew to an end, artificial islands, or crannogs, low thick-walled structures called duns, and lofty tower-like brochs appeared. When the Christian era dawned, the tribesmen and women sheltering within these defences faced a new threat.

Romans, Picts and Britons

In AD 79, Agricola, under orders from Emperor Vespasian, entered
north Britain with his legions and reached the River Tay. Four years later,
at the bloody battle of Mons Graupius (an eighteenth-century
misreading gave us the name Grampian), they defeated a confederation
of tribes they called the Caledonians. The country lay at Rome's mercy,
but for whatever reason Rome never grasped its prize.

Among the Caledonian warrior-chiefs was one called Calgacus. His is
the first name to appear in Scottish history. With the coming of the
Romans, Scotland steps from prehistory into history. We learn from
them the names of rivers, of mountains, of settlements. We learn also
that 16 tribes inhabited Scotland. Those in the north remained
implacably opposed to Rome throughout the four centuries of attempted
occupation; from them would emerge the tribal federation the Romans
called *Picti,* 'the painted people', and which we know as the Picts. What
they called themselves we may never know.

The southern tribes, like the Damnonii, from around the Firth of
Clyde, and the Votadini of Lothian, more fully under the Roman yoke,

*THE ANTONINE WALL
at BAR HILL,
Dunbartonshire.
Looking towards the River
Forth and the eastern end
of Imperial Rome's
northernmost frontier, built
in AD 142. The line of the
ditch and bank construction
can be seen stretching
across the landscape.*

*DUNADD FORT, Argyll.
This rocky fortress was a
royal residence of the kings
of the Scots of Dalriada, in
the sixth century.*

tolerated the invader. But these tribes too would re-emerge after the fall
of Rome with new identities: the Britons of Strathclyde, centred on the
volcanic rock of Dumbarton; and the Gododdin, whose chief place,
Traprain Law, in East Lothian, remains as monumentally impressive
today as it ever was.

The might of Rome, in contrast, has all but faded from the
landscape. Fine stretches of the Antonine Wall, the Empire's northernmost frontier built across central Scotland in 142 but abandoned within
a generation, survive; so too do the robust banks and ditches of their fort
at Ardoch, in Perthshire. But of the mighty legionary fortress at
Newstead, built in the shadow of the great tribal hillfort on Eildon Hill
North, near Melrose, nothing visible remains at all.

Coming of the Scots

By the year 400 the invader had become the invaded as repeated attacks
were made on, and beyond, Hadrian's Wall by the Picts and the Britons.
But new threats were also confronting the native tribes.

*ST COLUMBA'S
WINDOW, Iona Abbey.
William Wilson's stained
glass (1965) depicts the holy
man of God – Colum Cille,
'dove of the church' – who
in 597 passed away
peacefully at the island
monastery on Iona, which
he had founded in 563.*

Fighting alongside the Picts in those final years of Roman rule was a
people called the *Scotti*, the Scots. They were not native to the land but
newcomers from across the Irish Sea. Tradition has it that the Scots,
under their leader Fergus Mor, 'Fergus the Great', crossed from Antrim
in about the year 500 and settled in Argyll, but it seems more likely that
the Scots' migration to the land that now bears their name began around
the time of the Roman withdrawal. By 600 their kingdom of Dalriada

COLUM CILLE

Remember in the LORD
the Rev. Kenneth Macleod
D.D. Pastor and Bard

So Long as the Songs
of the Gael are Sung
this name will
endure 1873-1955

W. WILSON. 1965.

*URQUHART CASTLE
AND LOCH NESS,
Inverness-shire.
The rocky promontory
where this medieval castle
now stands was once the
residence of a Pictish
nobleman, Emchath, who
with his son, Virolec, and
his entire household were
baptised by St Columba.*

extended from the Mull of Kintyre to the mountains of Ardnamurchan. The Scots brought with them to the Highlands a new Celtic language, Gaelic (the name Argyll comes from *Earra Ghaidheal*, 'coastland of the Gael'); they also brought a new religion, Christianity, through the person of Saint Columba. From his island monastery on Iona, Columba made several missions into Pictland to spread the word of God. It was during one such mission, to the court of King Brude beside the River Ness, that he saved a companion from the jaws of a fierce water-beast, our first recorded sighting of the monster we now know better as 'Nessie'.

Christianity had previously come to the Britons, for Saint Ninian had established his missionary base at Whithorn, in Wigtownshire, in the fifth century. In the little museum there is the Latinus Stone, the earliest Christian memorial in Scotland.

Angles and Vikings
Columba passed peacefully away on Iona in 597. Already a new aggressor was emerging from the south to threaten the northern kingdoms of Picts, Scots and Britons. The Angles, a German race, were by now firmly

established in the north-east of the country that came to be named England after them.

In about the year 600, Mynyddog, king of the Gododdin, and his war-band set out from the rocky fortress of Din Eidyn to confront them, but suffered humiliating defeat. The Scots, judging that attack was the best form of defence, did likewise in 603, and failed too. The Angles, emboldened by these victories, sought for further riches in the north and in 638 besieged and captured Din Eidyn, which they renamed Edinburgh. The age of the Gododdin was over.

The Angles did not stop there. They penetrated deep into Galloway, and pushed northward into Pictland. But they over-reached themselves and in 685 King Ecgfrith of Northumbria and most of his army were slaughtered by the Picts at Nechtansmere, near the modern village of Dunnichen, in Angus; the wonderful Pictish carved stone in the churchyard at Aberlemno, six miles to the north of the battle site, depicts a battle scene, perhaps King Bridei's victory over Ecgfrith. The Angles had no option but to retreat from Pictland and re-establish the River Forth as their northern border.

The Anglian menace encouraged closer political dialogue between the threatened Picts, Scots and Britons. It is a confusing web of inter-relationships between the royal dynasties – King Bridei himself was a Strathclyde Briton and not a Pict – only finally resolved around 843 when Kenneth mac Alpin, king

SCONE PALACE, Perth. Here, on the Moot Hill (below), the Kings of the Picts and the Scots were enthroned on the Stone of Destiny. In 1296 Edward I removed the Stone to England (the one shown is a replica) – 700 years later it was finally returned and is now at Edinburgh Castle.

of the Scots, became king of the Picts also. The history of Pictland was over; Scotland was born.

Kenneth died in 858 not in his native Argyll but in the green and pleasant Earn valley near Perth. The Scottish Church also moved, from Iona to Dunkeld in the heart of Pictland; and the grassy knoll at Scone, The Moot Hill, where the Picts had proclaimed their kings, now became the inauguration place for the monarchs of the new united kingdom, who were set on the Stone of Destiny at enthronements.

The Scots' migration eastward may have been forced on them by the piratical raids of the Vikings from Norway. The first raid was made on Iona in 795; further raids followed in quick succession. Soon, the children of these summer raiders began to settle around the northern and western coasts and a powerful Norse earldom developed in Orkney and Caithness. But the Norwegian sway in the west proved not so overwhelming, and despite a Viking assault on Dumbarton Rock in 870, after which 200 longships carried the booty and the prisoners back to Dublin, the Norsemen never managed to establish themselves in Strathclyde.

JEDBURGH ABBEY (opposite) AND MELROSE ABBEY, Roxburghshire. Two of the four great Border abbeys built during the reign of King David I (1124-1153). The others were Kelso and Dryburgh. Whilst the 'black canons' at Jedburgh excelled at medicine, the 'white monks' of Melrose became successful sheep farmers.

*ST ANDREWS, Fife.
In the Middle Ages,
St Andrews was Scotland's
premier cathedral city and a
major pilgrimage place. Its
great cathedral (foreground)
was the largest church in
the land, and the
archbishop's castle (top
right) amongst the strongest
of fortresses. The town's
university, Scotland's oldest,
was founded by Bishop
Wardlaw in 1412.*

Medieval Scotland

By 1000 Scotland was a confusing miscellany of races – Britons, Scots,
Angles and Norse. But the Anglian hold over Lothian was fast slipping
from their grasp, and the Scottish King Malcolm II's victory at Carham,
on the Tweed, in 1018, effectively sealed the fate of these Englishmen.
In the same year Malcolm set his grandson, Duncan, on the throne of
Strathclyde, and when Malcolm died in 1034 Duncan, Macbeth's
predecessor, succeeded in integrating the ancient British kingdom of
Strathclyde into the realm of Scotland.

The Celtic blood coursed through the veins of Duncan's son,
Malcolm III, but from the moment he set eyes on the saintly Saxon
princess, Margaret, he was besotted. They married at Dunfermline about
1070 and she bore him eight children. The youngest boy, David, was
destined to bring Scotland out from its Celtic shadow and into the full
light of medieval Europe.

On the highest point of Edinburgh Castle is St Margaret's Chapel; it
is the oldest building in that royal fortress, indeed the oldest building in
Edinburgh. It was built by King David in remembrance of his mother,

who had died in the castle in 1093 of a broken heart grieving for her husband. David built many churches throughout his realm, from tiny parish kirks to towering abbeys. He also built castles as centres of government, and established towns as the focus of settlement and trade. His reign was of momentous significance for Scotland, but what had set David on this path?

David was born about 1080 in Dunfermline, but as a young lad travelled to the English court for the wedding of his sister Matilda to the future Henry I. There he remained, observing the feudal ways of the Normans. He married a rich Norman widow, Maud, and by the time of his return, in 1113, he was imbued with the feudal spirit. The changes he initiated, continued by his grandsons, Malcolm IV 'the Maiden', and William I 'the Lion', transformed the country; few aspects of life escaped.

These achievements were made possible only through the introduction of new blood. There wasn't a Norman conquest of Scotland as such, like there had been of England. But there was certainly a tidal wave of Norman immigration throughout the twelfth century, principally the sons of Norman and Breton noblemen residing in England, but including others, like sheep-farmers from Flanders.

The legacy of these immigrants lives on in many Scottish surnames, like Bruce, Lindsay, Sinclair, and most

ST CLEMENTS CHURCH, Rodel, Harris. An early 16th-century kirk built by Alasdair Crotach MacLeod, Lord of Dunvegan and Harris.

CROSS AT ORONSAY PRIORY, Argyll. Built by Colinus MacDuffie in the late 15th century.

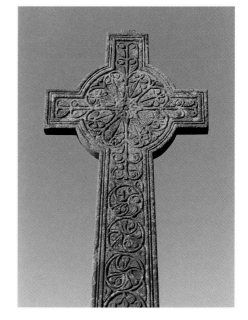

CAERLAVEROCK CASTLE, Dumfriesshire. The 13th-century fortress residence of the chief of the Maxwells was the scene of a mighty siege by England's King Edward I in the summer of 1300, during the height of the first 'War of Independence'.

famous of all, Stewart, the ancestors of the British royal house of Stewart.

It was Walter, the High Stewart, who in 1164 killed Somerled in battle near Renfrew. Somerled, of Celto-Norse stock, was Lord of the Isles and his death marked the beginning of the end of Norse dominion in the west.

By 1200, Alan Stewart, Walter's son, had taken Bute, the first island to fall to Scotland, and it was within sight of his castle at Rothesay, in the Firth of Clyde off Largs, that Hakon IV of Norway was repulsed in 1263. Retreating north, he breathed his last in the bishop's palace in Orkney. It proved also the last breath for Norwegian supremacy in the west and in 1266 King Magnus and King Alexander III signed the Treaty of Perth which brought Argyll and the Hebrides finally under Scottish rule.

The Wars of Independence

King Alexander's reign was called a 'golden age' by those living a century later, who had endured the horrors of the bloody and prolonged wars with England, the so-called 'Wars of Independence'. To them the thirteenth century was a time of peace and prosperity. But all that came to a brutal end on 30 March 1296, when Edward I of England crossed the Tweed and butchered most of the population of Berwick, Scotland's chief town and port. Edward 'Longshanks' was beginning to earn his other nickname 'Hammer of the Scots'. King John Balliol's short, sad reign (1292–96) was over.

Edward's chances of conquering Scotland certainly looked promising. His large army, battle-hardened from campaigning in Wales and France, faced 'the host', Scotland's common army of townsmen and countryfolk. Without a king, they found a leader not among the ranks of the senior nobility but in William Wallace, son of a Clydesdale laird. Wallace emerged from the shadows to carry the torch of Scottish freedom and, within a year of killing the English constable of Lanark Castle, won a remarkable victory at Stirling Bridge in September 1297. The outcome brought fresh hope to a nation staring into the abyss.

THE WALLACE MONUMENT, Abbey Craig, Stirling. A Victorian memorial to the legendary medieval hero William Wallace, who is said to have directed his great victory, the Battle of Stirling Bridge in 1297, from the same summit.

Wallace tasted defeat at Falkirk in the following year, but far worse was to follow. After a determined rearguard action he was betrayed and captured near Glasgow in 1305. A humiliating and cruel torture at the hands of Edward Plantagenet, in which he was dragged through the streets of London, hanged, cut down while still alive and disembowelled, saw a courageous man die but a national hero born.

The great nobleman who assumed Wallace's mantle was Robert the Bruce, Earl of Carrick, whose grandfather, also Robert, had been a

STIRLING CASTLE
Within sight of the castle, at the Battle of Bannockburn in 1314, Robert the Bruce (below) defeated the English King Edward II to secure Scotland's independence.

contender for the throne in 1292. Bruce now seized his chance and was crowned with a 'circlet of gold' at Scone on Easter Day, 1306.

The early days did not bode well. Defeat near Perth was followed by over a year in hiding. When he reappeared, reinvigorated for the cause of Scottish independence, he shrewdly adopted a 'scorched-earth' tactic against the oppressor until at last, on Mid-summer's Day 1314, he felt strong enough to meet the might of the English army head on. Bruce's defeat of Edward II at Bannockburn, near Stirling, ranks amongst the world's greatest battle victories.

The unassailable king reigned for 15 more years. When he passed peacefully away at his manor of Cardross, near Dumbarton, his heart was taken from his chest and carried on crusade. His bones were laid to rest in the royal mausoleum in Dunfermline Abbey.

Bruce's death was the signal for renewed English aggression and the country was plunged into a second 'War of Independence'. For 20 more bitter years the struggle between Scotland and England went on, during which John Balliol's son, Edward, crowned himself at Scone, and Bruce's son, David, the rightful king, was captured near Durham. Only with David's return from captivity in 1357 can the Wars of Independence be truly said to have ended.

The Royal House of Stewart

David Bruce died childless in 1371 and Bruce's grandson, Robert Stewart, ascended the throne as Robert II, the first of the royal house of Stewart. The dynasty lasted for over three centuries. During that time, three of her monarchs died fighting the English, two were murdered by their noblemen, two were beheaded, and one forced into exile. It reads as one long tale of woe, but it was far from so.

The splendid royal palaces at Falkland, Linlithgow and Stirling testify to their majesty, and two historical achievements stand out: in 1468, Scotland grew to its present extent when James III acquired the Northern Isles from Norway; and the ultimate achievement, unthinkable in the time of Bruce, was the accession in 1603 to the English throne of James VI. One might almost have heard the 'Hammer of the Scots' turning in his grave.

But it is the short, ill-starred reign of Mary Stuart, who used the French spelling of 'Stewart', that holds our attention 400 years on, perhaps because it has all the ingredients of a great novel – romance, intrigue, tragedy. It is a story that never tires in the telling.

THE FIRTH AND SANDSOUND VOE, Shetland.
The marriage in 1469 of King James III of Scotland and Margaret, daughter of Christian I of Norway and Denmark, brought both Shetland and Orkney into the realm of Scotland.

*THE OUTER GATE,
LINLITHGOW PALACE,
West Lothian.
These coats of arms are of
the four orders of chivalry to
which King James V
belonged: the Garter of
England, the Thistle of
Scotland, the Golden Fleece
of Burgundy and St
Michael of France.
Both James V (10 April
1512) and his daughter,
Mary Queen of Scots
(8 December 1542), were
born here in this residence
of the Stewart monarchs.*

Mary Queen of Scots

Mary was born in 1542 at Linlithgow Palace. Within a week her father, James V, was dead and she queen. Henry VIII of England, spying an opportunity, proposed that Mary marry his son, the future Edward VI, and he sent his army to Scotland to do the wooing. The 'War of the Rough Wooing' was as bitterly fought as anything witnessed during the Wars of Independence.

The Scots were not persuaded by such tactics and in 1548 Mary was smuggled to France. There she grew into an elegant young lady. Her beauty attracted the eye of the Dauphin, Francis, and in 1558 they were wed. Soon tragedy struck. First, her father-in-law, King Henry, died and Mary found herself Queen of France. Then her husband died. Mary, Queen of France for barely 18 months, was a widow at the age of 17. She decided to return home and in August 1561 she landed at Leith, near Edinburgh.

The six years of her Scottish reign were tempestuous. They were not entirely of Mary's making; the Reformation of the Church in 1560 had sent shock waves through the realm which Mary was powerless to calm.

But Mary's own faults and misjudgements, combined with the growing religious and political unrest, proved disastrous. Her Catholic leanings led not only to arguments with John Knox, the fiery Protestant preacher, but also to disquiet among her noblemen. Her second marriage, to Henry Lord Darnley, in 1565, went horribly wrong, firstly with the murder of her Italian secretary, David Riccio, then with the death in mysterious circumstances of Darnley himself. By now Mary was besotted by the Earl of Bothwell and risked both her health and her reputation for him when she rode out from Jedburgh across the bleak Border countryside to visit him at his castle of Hermitage. They married soon after Darnley's demise.

HERMITAGE CASTLE, Roxburghshire. In the autumn of 1566, Mary Queen of Scots visited her beloved Patrick Hepburn, fourth Earl of Bothwell, as he lay injured at his fortress in deepest Liddesdale.

Mary's dalliance with Bothwell proved her undoing and she was arrested by her nobles in June 1567 and imprisoned in the island fortress of Lochleven, near Kinross. There, on 24 July, she was compelled to abdicate in favour of her only son, James. The birth of an heir, in a tiny closet room inside Edinburgh Castle in June 1556, had been the one ray of sunshine in an otherwise storm-ridden reign.

Mary eventually escaped from her watery prison and fled to England.

EDINBURGH CASTLE stands on the site of a 340-million-year-old volcano, occupied by man since the Bronze Age. By the later Middle Ages, it had become Scotland's premier royal castle housing the national records, the royal artillery and the Crown, Sceptre and Sword of State.

THE PASS OF KILLIECRANKIE, Perthshire. (opposite) Here beside the River Garry on 27 July 1689, the Jacobites, led by Viscount Dundee, routed the army of Protestant William and Mary. In the very hour of his victory, 'Bonnie Dundee' fell mortally wounded and the supporters of the exiled King James VII, suddenly bereft of their great leader, failed to drive home their advantage.

There she endured a further 20 years as a virtual prisoner of her cousin, Queen Elizabeth, until in 1587, the 'Virgin Queen', wearying of the continuing intrigue that surrounded Mary, ordered her execution. It was the final dramatic act in a tragedy of a life.

Union of the Crowns

When Elizabeth died in 1603, Mary's son, James VI, rode south to become James I of England also. But the Union of the Crowns proved no panacea for the nation's ills and the seventeenth century was as troubled as any that had gone before. Religion in particular set king against country, clan against clan, family against family. Among the victims was Charles I, executed by the English in 1649. But it was the Scots who first quarrelled with Charles when, in 1637, Jenny Geddes threw her stool at the bishops in the High Kirk of St Giles, in Edinburgh's Royal Mile, in protest at the introduction of the Prayer Book and sparked a riot. The National Covenant, declared in the following year, fanned the flame of civil war.

Civil war was followed by Cromwell's invasion of 1650 and 10 years of rule from England. Charles II, the last monarch to be crowned in Scotland, at Scone on New Year's Day 1651, returned to his throne in 1660 only to re-open the religious wounds. The conflict between king and covenanter came to be known as the 'killing time'. His death in 1685, and the flight into exile four years later of his even more avowedly Catholic brother, James VII, failed to stem the flow of blood. When the

Protestant William and Mary were proclaimed joint sovereigns of Scotland in April 1689, Jacobitism (from 'Jacobus', Latin for James) was born. Perhaps if 'Bonnie Dundee' (James Graham of Claverhouse, Viscount Dundee), the Jacobite commander at the Battle of Killiecrankie, fought in July of that year, had not been mortally wounded in the moment of his victory, the course of Scottish history might have been very different.

A United Kingdom

On 16 January 1707, Parliament, meeting in Edinburgh's Royal Mile, passed its final piece of legislation, the Act of Union. As Chancellor Seafield lifted up the royal sceptre to touch the parchment over which the members had debated so bitterly for so long, he uttered the immortal words: 'Now, there's ane end of ane auld sang'. The sceptre was then taken with the other Honours of Scotland, the Crown and the mighty Sword of State, back to the strongroom in Edinburgh Castle and locked away. These ancient royal regalia, amongst the oldest in Europe, had no further use, for that final act saw Scotland merge with England to

EILEAN DONAN CASTLE
This ancient MacKenzie stronghold beside Loch Duich, was garrisoned by the Jacobites in June 1719 before their defeat in the nearby Pass of Glenshiel at the hands of General Wightman's redcoats.

GLENCOE (opposite), where in the early hours of 13 February 1692, 38 men, women and children of the MacDonald clan were slaughtered by redcoats garrisoned at nearby Fort William. This atmospheric glen has become known as the 'Glen of Weeping'.

GLAMIS CASTLE, Angus. The 'Old Pretender', Bonnie Prince Charlie's father, who stayed there in January 1716, later declared that he had seen no finer edifice. It was the childhood home of Queen Elizabeth, the Queen Mother, and is said to be the most haunted castle in Scotland.

GLENFINNAN MONUMENT, Lochaber. (opposite) The 60 ft-high monument at the head of Loch Shiel, topped with the figure of a clansman, was raised by Alexander MacDonald of Glenaladale in 1815 to commemorate the start here of the last Jacobite Rising in 1745.

become the United Kingdom of Great Britain and Ireland. Henceforth, the British Parliament would meet in London. Scottish history now became British history.

The Treaty of Union might have united the two nations, but it brought great division in Scotland. Amid the tensions in society, the embers of Jacobitism were fanned into life once more. An abortive landing on the Fife coast by James VIII, the 'Old Pretender', in 1708 was followed by a far more threatening uprising in 1715, which might have succeeded in returning a Stewart to the British throne had its military leader, the Earl of Mar, not been so inept a commander. Thirty years on, the Pretender's son, Bonnie Prince Charlie, landed on Eriskay, in the Western Isles, to begin another uprising which saw him reach almost to the gates of London itself. But his retreat from Derby ended in humiliating defeat on the bloody battlefield of Culloden where Prince Charles saw his brave Highland army fall before the Hanoverian guns. That defeat, in April 1746, sounded the death-knell for the ancient House of Stewart. Culloden was the last battle fought on British soil.

This faltering start to the new Great Britain in time gave way to renewed optimism, and as the economic benefits of union began to be felt, the Scots found new energies and dynamism, so strong that the later eighteenth century has been christened the 'Age of Enlightenment'. This was the age of David Hume and Adam Smith, of Robert Adam, Thomas Telford and James Watt, of Robert Burns and Walter Scott. It was the age which saw the countryside transformed through agricultural

CHARLOTTE SQUARE,
Edinburgh,
part of James Craig's New
Town plan, was designed by
Robert Adam and
completed by 1820.

ABBOTSFORD HOUSE,
near Melrose, Borders.
The home of Sir Walter
Scott (1771-1832), noted
novelist and antiquarian.

improvements, and Edinburgh blossom forth with the building of her spectacular Georgian New Town. It also saw Scotland give to the world a remarkable number of 'firsts', including the first post office and the first savings bank. For such a small country, Scotland's contribution to the world has been immense.

This vitality and inventiveness continued throughout the nineteenth century and ensured that Scotland was at the forefront of the momentous changes that now made Great Britain the world's leading industrial nation. There was no sphere of human endeavour, be it medicine, science, engineering, exploration or the arts, where the Scots could not claim to have distinguished themselves: chloroform, the magnetic compass, the telephone, even the humble bicycle, joined that ancient invention, whisky, in the country's 'hall of fame'.

But nineteenth-century Scotland had its dark side too. In 1843, the Church of Scotland tore itself apart at the Disruption when more than half its ministers and congregations left their manses and churches to create the Free Church.

There was, too, the dreadful exploitation of their workers by the coal owners and factory bosses, which led to the formation of the Scottish Labour Party in 1888 by a Lanarkshire man, Keir Hardie, who had himself been sent down the pit at the age of 10.

But perhaps most cruel of all were the Highland Clearances of the beginning of the century, during which many thousands of men, women and children were ruthlessly evicted by their landlords from their homes in the straths and glens and left to find a new life wherever they could. Many moved south to the growing industrial cities and towns in the Lowlands, but countless more emigrated to Canada and America, and later to Australia and New Zealand. Onto their abandoned crofts came the cheviot and the stag.

In 1890, the Forth Rail Bridge was officially opened by the Prince of Wales. A monument to the three pillars of the Victorian economy – coal, iron and the railway – it was the culmination of a half-century of

industrial supremacy which saw Scotland's products, like ships, railway locomotives and textiles, dispersed throughout the world. But even as the Prince's train was chugging across 'the eighth wonder of the world', the country's great industries were in decline. The outbreak of the Great War in 1914 brought about some respite for the once mighty shipyards and steelworks, but at an enormous cost. Of the 500,000 Scots who enlisted

SUTHERLAND
One of the many highland landscapes left bare after the Clearances.

THE VILLAGE, HIRTA, ST KILDA
The last 36 inhabitants of the remote islands of St Kilda, 50 miles west of Harris, were evacuated in 1930, ending over 4000 years of human occupation.

*GLENFINNAN
VIADUCT, on the
West Highland Line,
completed in 1901.*

*THE FORTH RAIL
BRIDGE. (opposite)
Opened in 1890, John
Fowler and Benjamin
Baker's masterpiece is an
icon of Scotland's proud
industrial heritage.*

*FINNIESTON QUAY
CRANE, Glasgow.
Built in 1931 and
landmark of a bygone era.*

in the armed forces, a fifth never returned home. Despite the hopes and expectations of those fortunate enough to survive 'the war to end all wars', the misery continued in the war's wake, with social deprivation and mass unemployment around the factories and yards which once drove the industrial revolution.

It took the outbreak of the Second World War in 1939 to bring the nation together once more. Since that time Scotland has experienced something of a revival, both at work and at play – remember, the first British side to lift the European Cup was Celtic Football Club, in 1967 – a rejuvenation which has been brought about by those same qualities of skill, endeavour and inventiveness which have long been the hallmark of her people.

There have been many enterprising Scots down the centuries, among them scientists, philosophers, politicians – some well-known, countless others unknown. In a quiet East Lothian graveyard lie the mortal remains of one whose name is not so often on folks' lips, Andrew Meikle. In the 1780s this humble mill engineer perfected the threshing machine, whose motion beats at the heart of every modern combine harvester. It is an invention people all over the world have benefited from, one of which our first neolithic farmers, tilling the land 6000 years earlier, would have been justly proud.

RUTHVEN BARRACKS, Strathspey, Inverness-shire, built in the aftermath of the 1715 Jacobite rising on the site of a medieval castle of the Lords of Badenoch.

OIL RIGS: A common sight in the North Sea since the development of the offshore oil industry in the 1960s and '70s